Introduction

We Both Read books can be read alone or with another person. If you are reading the book alone, you can read it like any other book. If you are reading with another person, you can take turns reading aloud. If you are taking turns, the reader with more experience should read the parts marked with a yellow dot ⬤. The reader with less experience should read the parts marked with a blue dot ⬤. As you read, you will notice some difficult words introduced in sections with a yellow dot, then repeated in sections with a blue dot. You can recognize these words by their **bold lettering**.

Sharing the reading of a book can be a lot of fun, and reading aloud is a great way to improve fluency and expression. If you are reading with someone else, you might also want to take the time, while reading the book, to interact and talk about what is happening in the story. After reading with someone else, you might even want to experience reading the entire book on your own.

The Oprah Winfrey Story
We Both Read® Chapter Book

Text Copyright © 2009 by Lisa Maria and Treasure Bay, Inc.
Illustrations Copyright © 2009 by Marc Scott
All rights reserved

We Both Read® is a trademark of Treasure Bay, Inc.

With special thanks to Angela DePaul of Harpo Productions
for her comments and suggestions.

Published by Treasure Bay, Inc.
P.O. Box 2665
San Anselmo, CA 94979

PRINTED IN SINGAPORE

Library of Congress Control Number: 2009924400

Hardcover ISBN-13: 978-1-60115-241-1
Paperback ISBN-13: 978-1-60115-242-8

We Both Read® Books
Patent No. 5,957,693

Visit us online at:
www.webothread.com

WE BOTH READ®

The Oprah Winfrey Story

By Lisa Maria and Sindy McKay
Illustrations by Marc Scott

Contents

CHAPTER 1	"O" Is for Oprah	2
CHAPTER 2	Life on the Farm	4
CHAPTER 3	Back and Forth	12
CHAPTER 4	Keep Turning the Page	20
CHAPTER 5	Each Day Is a Wonder	26
CHAPTER 6	Welcome to Chicago	32
CHAPTER 7	The Biggest Adventure	34

TREASURE BAY

Chapter 1
"O" Is for Oprah

"When you get the chance, go for it."
OPRAH WINFREY

Many of us know Oprah Winfrey from her incredibly popular talk show, *The Oprah Winfrey Show.* However, Oprah does much more than simply host a talk show. She is also a brilliant producer and an **inspired** actress who donates time and money to many different charities around the world.

One of Oprah's many goodwill projects was Christmas Kindness South Africa 2002. More than fifty thousand poor children in South Africa received gifts of food, clothing, athletic shoes, books, and toys. The children adored Oprah and lovingly nicknamed her "Mama Oprah."

Oprah loves sharing her good fortune with others and she loves giving surprises. One day, Oprah surprised the guests on her show by giving each one of them a new car!

Most people would say that Oprah works in television, but Oprah feels that her real job is helping people to understand one another. She hopes to **inspire** people to help others, take chances, and live their "best life."

Oprah believes that everyone is important and deserves to be treated with respect. Many people are treated poorly because of where they come from, how much money they have, or the color of their skin. Oprah often has guests on her show who have faced these challenges. She has faced some pretty big challenges herself.

Chapter 2
Life on the Farm

*"Whenever you've been touched by love,
a heart-print lingers, so that you're always reminded
of the feeling of being cared for."*
Oprah Winfrey

Oprah Winfrey was born on January 29, 1954, in the southern state of Mississippi. At that time, the South was still segregated. That means that some people believed that white and black people should be kept apart. There were separate schools for white and black children and separate neighborhoods for white and black families. There were even separate restaurants, restrooms, and water fountains. Some white people were cruel and hurt African-Americans and called them names. Many African-Americans could not get a good education or a decent job. This kind of behavior is called "**racism.**" Oprah's family struggled with racism.

Her family also struggled with poverty. Oprah's parents were young and poor when she was born. Her mother realized she couldn't take good care of Oprah, so she made a tough decision. She decided to leave young Oprah with Oprah's grandparents for awhile.

Oprah's grandparents owned a farm in Mississippi. Her great-great-grandparents had been slaves and had bought this land when they were freed after the Civil War.

When Oprah was three years old, her grandmother, Hattie Mae, began to teach her to read, write, and do math. She believed that, because of **racism**, Oprah would need to be well educated if she was to succeed.

Many years later, Oprah would declare, "My grandmother really raised me to be who I am because of her belief in education."

Oprah and her grandparents worked very hard on their farm, but they never made much money. They ate whatever they could grow, and the clothes they wore were all handmade by Oprah's grandmother. To save money, Oprah's grandmother took care of Oprah's hair. She trimmed it herself and often braided it into two pigtails. Oprah hated having her hair brushed and braided. It hurt when her grandmother accidentally pulled too hard!

Oprah shared her grandmother's room and slept with her under a pile of warm handmade quilts. The only bathroom they had was an outhouse: a small building near the house with a toilet inside. She took a bath once a week in a washing tub in the kitchen with water that was heated on the stove.

Oprah had many chores on the farm. There was no running water in the house, so every day, Oprah carried two buckets down to the well to draw water. Carrying the buckets to the well was easy. Carrying them back was not. The full buckets were very heavy!

It was also Oprah's job to feed and care for the pigs, cows, and chickens.

To make her chores go faster, Oprah often sang songs she had learned in church. Sometimes she even made up songs of her own to sing as she worked.

Oprah didn't have any friends to play with on the farm, so when she finished her chores, she played with the animals. Her grandmother had taught her to read at an early age, so Oprah also entertained herself by reading books. She often read out loud to her animal friends.

Oprah's gift for speaking and performing started early. Oprah loved the feel and the sound of the words rolling off her tongue. She would stand on hay bales in the barn and read story after story, acting out all the different parts and using a different voice for each character.

There was no money to spend on toys, so Oprah made her own doll from a **corncob**. (The "cob" is what's left after the good part of an ear of corn is eaten.)

Oprah loved her **corncob** doll. She took good care of it and made sure it was safe from any hungry pigs. Today, Oprah enjoys collecting dolls of all types, especially black dolls.

If you think it's hard to imagine not having any toys, try to imagine not having a television! Oprah's grandparents could not afford such a luxury. In fact, they didn't even have electricity. But Oprah didn't seem to mind. She kept herself busy reading, playing, and helping her grandmother.

Oprah's grandmother insisted that her young granddaughter show good manners, and she made sure that Oprah studied hard. She believed that these habits would take Oprah far in life. As it turns out, she was right!

On Sundays, she brought Oprah to church, and Oprah would read and recite Bible verses. The adults in the church loved listening to little Oprah and were impressed by her presence and strong voice. The church ladies in their big hats would fan themselves and give approving nods to Oprah's grandmother, saying, "Hattie Mae, this child is gifted! She sure can talk!"

Oprah did all of this before she was even old enough to go to **kindergarten**.

When Oprah finally did go to **kindergarten**, she was far more advanced than her fellow students. She sent a note to her teacher that said, "Dear Miss New, I do not think I belong here." Her teacher agreed and skipped Oprah ahead to the first grade.

Because of this, some of the other children thought Oprah was a show-off. They were mean to her and called her names. This was hard for Oprah. She wanted friends, but she also liked being smart. Oprah decided to stay true to herself. She kept learning and later even went on to skip another grade.

Chapter 3
Back and Forth

"You are not your circumstances.
You are your possibilities.
If you know that, you can do anything."
OPRAH WINFREY

When Oprah was six years old, her mother was ready for Oprah to come live with her again. Oprah wasn't sure she wanted to leave her grandmother's farm. She barely remembered her mother, who was now living in the northern state of Wisconsin. Oprah, however, had no choice in the matter and was sent to her mother's home.

By now, Oprah's mother had another daughter and an infant son. The four of them lived together in a tiny, **cockroach**-infested apartment in a poor, busy neighborhood. The two girls were treated differently. Oprah's half-sister was allowed to sleep in the house with her mother, while Oprah had to sleep on the porch.

Oprah's mother left for work early in the morning and didn't return home until late at night. Her two **daughters** were left alone every day after school.

Oprah was terribly bored at her mother's house. She and her sister didn't get along well. Since her mother was always working, she didn't have any time to spend with her **daughters**. Oprah felt very alone. But instead of feeling sorry for herself, Oprah found some new and different friends—a couple of **cockroaches**! She named them Melinda and Sandy and she had a lot of fun trying to get them to race.

Oprah's mother kept her for three years. Then, worn out from working and taking care of her three children, she called Oprah's father for help.

Oprah's father and his current wife lived in Nashville, Tennessee. They had no other children and were thrilled to take young Oprah into their home. They knew that she would thrive with love, attention, and rules.

Oprah started speaking at church again and her hard work paid off. Nine-year-old Oprah was asked to give a speech to a church group and was paid five hundred dollars!

Oprah knew that she was smart, but she was not confident about the way she looked. She didn't feel very pretty. And sometimes she felt that people didn't like the way she looked simply because she was black.

Then one day, an important woman came to visit Oprah's church. Her name was Tish Fort Hooker, and her husband was running for governor of Tennessee.

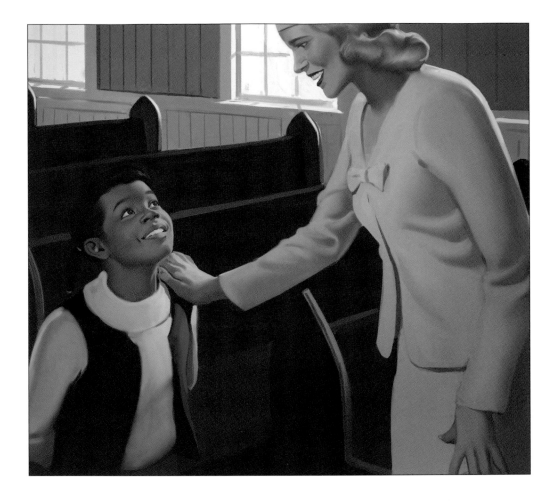

Mrs. Hooker smiled at Oprah and sweetly said, "My, you're as pretty as a speckled pup!" She told Oprah many times how lovely she looked. She helped Oprah to see that being black was wonderful and that she should be proud of being black. Oprah felt pretty for the first time in her life.

Oprah never forgot that moment. Years later, Tish Hooker was invited to surprise Oprah on her show. Oprah was thrilled to see her and to be able to thank her in person. She told her that those kind and thoughtful words, so long ago, had changed her life.

Unfortunately, Oprah began to have problems at school. Many kids were mean to her and picked on her because she was a good student.

Oprah's teacher was worried for her safety. He arranged for Oprah to enter a program that helped poor children go to better schools.

At her new school, the children admired Oprah for being a good student. Yet, she still felt out of place. The other children were from rich families. Oprah didn't have all the nice things her schoolmates had. Sadly, she started stealing and getting into trouble.

Oprah liked living at her father's house. She didn't seem to mind his strict rules, and she liked her new school. When summer arrived, Oprah's mother arranged for Oprah to come and stay with her. Oprah expected to go back to her father's home in the fall, but her mother decided to keep her instead. Oprah's father was upset and worried about Oprah.

His fears came true. Oprah had no one to take care of her while her mother was at work. Troublemakers harmed Oprah and told her to keep secrets. Oprah suffered because she kept those secrets for a long time. She felt alone and afraid, and she didn't believe that anyone would help her.

Today, Oprah asks children to tell their secrets to an adult so they can get help and be safe. If that adult doesn't help, she urges children to tell other adults until they get help. Oprah cares so much about children that she worked hard to get a law passed to help protect them. The law is informally known as "The Oprah Bill."

By the time Oprah was fourteen, she was in trouble all the time. She had even tried running away from home. She didn't feel like she belonged anywhere.

Her mother was angry and weary of Oprah's **behavior**. Not knowing what else to do, she decided to take Oprah to a home for troubled teens. She planned on leaving Oprah there that very day, but there were no beds available at the time. They were told to come back in two weeks.

Oprah's mother couldn't wait that long, so once again she called Oprah's father to come to the rescue. He quickly agreed to take Oprah and came immediately to bring his teenage daughter back home to Tennessee.

At first, it was hard for Oprah to be back with her father. She wasn't used to being watched so closely. She was used to doing whatever she wanted to do. Then, one day, her careless **behavior** landed her in the hospital. Finally, she was able to see that she was hurting herself and ruining her life. Staring at the hospital wall, Oprah realized that if she didn't change, she'd always be in trouble. She knew right then that she wanted to start over. She wanted to be an honest, loving, and helpful person. She wanted to live the kind of life she had read about in all her favorite books. She just didn't know how to begin.

Oprah gathered her courage and asked for help.

Chapter 4
Keep Turning the Page

"Reading . . . gives you the ability to reach higher ground. A world of possibilities awaits you. Keep turning the page."
OPRAH WINFREY

Oprah's father and stepmother felt that the best way to help Oprah succeed was to teach her healthy habits. She was given a curfew and a regular bedtime. She had to eat healthy meals and was not allowed to wear makeup or wear clothes that her parents thought were inappropriate. Oprah also had to go to church regularly and was given **responsibilities** around the house.

Her father insisted that she read at least one book every week—and write a book report about it! She was also expected to get good grades in school. Her father said that if she were a child who could only get C's, that would be okay. But Oprah could do better, so C's were not acceptable.

Oprah followed these strict rules. She knew they were good for her and she was grateful for her parents' help. Her joy of reading and learning returned, and she became an excellent student once more.

Today, Oprah believes that her love of reading "saved her life." Without learning to read, she would not have done well in school. Doing well in school gave Oprah more choices in life. Reading was the beginning of a new and better life for her.

For the first time in a long time, Oprah felt good about herself. Having **responsibilities** taught her to be a strong person. She was learning how to live a good life. People believed in Oprah again. She was not going to let them down. And she was not going to let herself down.

Oprah's high school in Nashville, Tennessee, was one of the first public schools to integrate in the South. This meant that blacks and whites were now allowed to go to school together.

Just as blacks and whites were striving to live together as equals, women and men were also working on issues of equality. When Oprah was young, most women were expected to stay home and take care of the house and the children. Some women, like Oprah's grandmother and mother, had two jobs: a job taking care of the family, plus a job working for money. Oprah's mother told her that the best job she could hope for would be to work as a maid for a good family. Oprah, however, would not accept such limitations, and she set her mind on going to college.

Oprah joined the Drama Club, became vice president of the Student Council, and was elected "Most Popular Girl" in her school. She competed in and won many speaking contests.

News of Oprah's speaking skills spread, and she was often asked to speak at churches and in front of civic groups. She even began to get paid for speaking. This made Oprah's father, and Oprah, very proud.

Oprah was becoming so good at public speaking that she was chosen to go to Washington D.C. for a national speaking competition. The competition was held in the White House—the President's own home! Only two students were chosen from the entire state of Tennessee to attend, and Oprah was one of them. It was a very exciting time for her, meeting other serious and hard-working students from all over the United States.

Things were really starting to go well for Oprah. She was thriving in every area of her life: home, school, and activities. She was respected for who she was and had lots of friends. Oprah was happy.

Now that everything was going so well, Oprah began to seriously consider what she wanted to do with the rest of her life. She thought she might like to travel to far away lands to help care for sick and needy people. Oprah also thought about becoming a teacher and helping children learn to read. She always cared about others. Helping people made her feel good.

Chapter 5
Each Day Is a Wonder

"... every sunrise is like a new page,
a chance to right ourselves and receive each day
in all its glory. Each day is a wonder."
OPRAH WINFREY

As Oprah grew older, she looked for more competitions where she could perform and win prizes. She even began entering beauty contests, hoping to win a college **scholarship** so that she could continue her education. During Nashville's Miss Fire Prevention pageant, the contestants were asked what they would do with a million dollars. Oprah gave the judges her bubbly smile and blurted out, "I'd be a spending fool!" Everyone laughed and voted for her. Oprah was the first black woman to win that pageant. She also won many other beauty contests, including Miss Black Tennessee.

Because of her talent, good grades, and contest wins, Oprah was starting to get noticed in the community. The manager of a local radio station, WVOL, thought it would be fun to have her visit the station and read into a microphone.

Oprah gave it a try. She did great! In fact, the manager at WVOL was so impressed that he hired her to read the news after school. At age seventeen, Oprah had her first broadcasting job.

Oprah also continued to enter speech competitions. At an Elk's Club speech contest, she won a full **scholarship** to Tennessee State University. Now, Oprah would get to go to college for free.

Oprah loved college. She studied speech and drama. While she was in her second year, the manager of a local Nashville TV station heard about a talented radio announcer named Oprah Winfrey. They offered her a job as co-anchor of their daytime news. Oprah took that job and became the first African-American woman to co-anchor the news in Nashville.

Oprah worked at the Nashville TV station for three years, while still going to college. Then a station in Baltimore, Maryland, offered Oprah an even better job. Only 22 years old, Oprah was asked to co-anchor Baltimore's *Six O'Clock News*.

Oprah wanted the job, but it meant she would have to leave college before **graduation**. She knew that would upset her father. She didn't know what to do, so she asked one of her professors for help.

OPRAH WINFREY

The professor spoke to Oprah's father and encouraged him to let her try the job. After all, she could always go back and finish college later. Finally, her father agreed and Oprah moved to Baltimore.

Later, Oprah did finish college. In 1987, more than ten years later, she received her degree from Tennessee State University. She was invited to give a speech at **graduation**. In her speech, she told her fellow graduates, ". . . this is a special day for my dad." She then announced that she was creating ten scholarships at the school in her father's name. This would allow other excellent, but poor, students to continue their education for free.

Oprah began her job at the TV station in Baltimore, Maryland—and it was a disaster! Her bosses at the station wanted Oprah to read the news in a serious, formal way. That just wasn't Oprah's style. She would laugh if she misread a word. If a story was sad, she couldn't help crying, like when a mother lost all seven of her children in a fire. Oprah cared about everyone she met.

The people at the station also began to criticize Oprah on her appearance. They didn't like it when she gained weight, and they insisted that she change her hairstyle. It wasn't long before Oprah was fired from her position on the news.

The station manager could fire Oprah from the news, but he had to find her another job. He asked Oprah to co-host a new local talk show. She said she was willing to try.

On the talk show, Oprah could finally just be herself. She loved talking to people and hearing their stories. And the audience loved her! Oprah had found the perfect job.

She still remembers what it felt like: "I said to myself, this is what I should be doing! It's like breathing."

Chapter 6
Welcome to Chicago

"The true meaning of courage to me is:
you're afraid—and then, with your knees knocking
and your heart racing—you step on out anyway."
Oprah Winfrey

After eight successful years in Baltimore, Oprah felt ready for something new. At about the same time, a woman who worked on her Baltimore show left for a job on a talk show in Chicago, Illinois. The woman soon learned that the Chicago show needed a new host, and she immediately thought of Oprah.

The possibility of a new job made Oprah so excited that she stayed up late that night creating a demo tape of her work. The demo tape included parts of different shows she had done, so the people at the station could see what she looked and sounded like on television. She sent the tape to the TV station and crossed her fingers.

The people at the TV station loved the tape and wanted her to come for an interview. Oprah was thrilled, but nervous. "Everybody, with the exception of my best friend, told me it wouldn't work. They said I was black, female, and overweight. They said that Chicago is a racist city and the talk-show formula was on its way out."

In spite of her fear, Oprah flew to Chicago for the interview, and she got the job! At the age of 29, Oprah became the new host of *A.M. Chicago.*

Oprah said that the first day on the air was the scariest day of her life. Again, in spite of her fear, Oprah did a fantastic job and was a big hit.

As her fame grew, Oprah's influence on the show grew. She chose the topics. She chose the guests. She chose the people who worked there. After one year, *A.M. Chicago* was renamed *The Oprah Winfrey Show.*

Chapter 7
The Biggest Adventure

"There is no greater calling than service to others.
And there is no better way to have your blessings multiply."
OPRAH WINFREY

One morning, Quincy Jones, a famous producer in the entertainment industry, happened to see Oprah on her TV show. He immediately knew that she would be perfect for a role in a movie called *The Color Purple*. He called her and asked her if she would try out for the part of Sofia.

Oprah could hardly believe her good fortune. *The Color Purple* was one of her all-time favorite books. She had even given it as a gift to many of her friends. Now she had a chance to be in the movie.

Oprah desperately wanted to play the part of Sofia, but it was scary to think of all the wonderful actresses she would be competing against. Once again, Oprah refused to let fear get in the way of her dream. She flew to Los Angeles and auditioned for the movie.

The filmmakers took a long time to decide who would play Sofia. Two months went by and Oprah was sure someone else must have gotten the role. She decided to go for a run, even though it was raining. Running always made her feel better. She ran hard and had a good cry. She began to sing a song from church, "I surrender, I surrender all . . ." Oprah decided to let go and accept whatever happened. At that instant, she received a phone call. She had gotten the part!

In 1985, Oprah was nominated for an Academy Award for Best Supporting Actress for her role of Sofia in *The Color Purple*. It was her first film.

Until 1986, *The Oprah Winfrey Show* only aired in the city of Chicago. The show went national at about the same time that *The Color Purple* came out in theaters.

The whole country fell in love with Oprah, and almost instantly, her show became the number one talk show in the United States. Over the years, *The Oprah Winfrey Show* has become the longest-running talk show in television history, and the **production** has won dozens of awards. Oprah has been nicknamed the "Queen of Daytime TV."

Oprah has said, "I'm grateful for my days of emptying slop jars, hauling water from the well, and going to the outhouse and thinking I was going to fall in. It makes walking through my house with the many bathrooms and marble floors and great view that much better."

Encouraged by her TV and film success, Oprah formed Harpo **Productions**, Inc., in 1988. (*Harpo* is *Oprah* spelled backwards!) Oprah started the company because she wanted to bring her favorite stories to life on the screen.

Oprah was only the third woman to own a major **production** company in the United States. The first was Mary Pickford, a famous film actress. The second was Lucille Ball, a very funny woman best known for her TV show, *I Love Lucy*.

Over the years, Oprah has produced and starred in many films for the big screen and TV.

On her talk show, Oprah has always done her best to inspire and uplift her viewers. In doing this, she has had the opportunity to interview some of the most important and famous people of our time.

Oprah loves books and has often said, "Books were my pass to personal freedom." So it's not surprising that she was inspired to create Oprah's Book Club as part of her talk show. Oprah's Book Club has motivated many people to read more and even to form their own book clubs to talk about the books they read.

Oprah has won many awards for her work, including being selected by *Time* magazine as one of the 100 Most Influential People of the 20th Century.

In 2000, she created *O, The Oprah Magazine.* It was one of the most successful magazine launches in history. Her magazine is much like her show. It features articles that help people improve their lives and the lives of others.

Oprah believes that "anybody can create miracles in the life of someone else." She formed Oprah's Angel Network as a way for people to work together to help others. Since then, Oprah's Angel Network has received millions of dollars in donations to help send students to college, build houses, and fulfill dreams.

In the words of Oprah: "Great things happen when people come together with an intention to create hope and opportunity."

Education is an important part of Oprah's mission. She donates money and books to schools all over the United States and has funded the building of libraries around the world. Using donations from Oprah's Angel Network, she has also had new schools built in more than a dozen countries.

In 2007, she created the Oprah Winfrey Leadership Academy for Girls in South Africa. The school gives disadvantaged girls a chance for a better life.

"Material success provides you with the ability to concentrate on the things that really matter," says Oprah. "And that is being able to make a difference, not only in your life, but in other people's lives."

Every day on her show, Oprah encourages people to live their "best life." Here are some tips from Oprah on how to do just that:

"Trust your instincts. Honor your own truth. Discern it, know it, and follow it."

"Insight, escape, information, knowledge, inspiration, power. All that and more can come through a good book."

"Life isn't just about what you can have; it's about what you have to give. What kind of person do you want to be?"

"The biggest adventure you can ever take is to live the life of your dreams."

To see all the We Both Read books that are available,
just go online to **www.webothread.com**